BLACKPOOL IN 50 BUILDINGS

CHRIS BOTTOMLEY & ALLAN W. WOOD

AMBERLEY

Blackpool Citadel, Salvation Army, Raikes Parade.

We would like to thank Michael D Beckwith, Gregg Wolstenholme, Blackpool Pleasure Beach, Historic England, Blackpool Entertainment Company Limited, Mark Spencer, the Institution of Civil Engineers and the Imperial Hotel for allowing us to use their photographs in the book. Thanks also to the late Ted Lightbown and Tony Sharkey for their assistance.

First published 2022

Amberley Publishing, The Hill, Stroud
Gloucestershire GL5 4EP

www.amberley-books.com

ISBN 978 1 4456 9938 7 (print)
ISBN 978 1 4456 9939 4 (ebook)

Typesetting by SJmagic DESIGN SERVICES, India.
Printed in Great Britain.

Contents

Key

1. Blackpool Tower
2. The Winter Gardens and Opera House, Church Street
3. The Three Piers
4. The Golden Mile
5. Stanley Park
6. The Pleasure Beach
7. Talbot Gateway, Talbot Road
8. The Sea Walls
9. Blackpool War Memorial (Cenotaph), Princess Parade
10. The Church of the Sacred Heart, No. 17 Talbot Road
11. Grand Theatre, No. 33 Church Street
12. The Shrine of Our Lady of Lourdes, Whinney Heys Road
13. Norbreck Castle Hotel, Queen's Promenade
14. Miners' Convalescent Home, Queen's Promenade
15. Shelters on the Promenade
16. Cabin Lift at the Boating Pool, Queen's Promenade
17. The Imperial Hotel, Promenade
18. Metropole Hotel, Promenade
19. Festival House, Promenade
20. Woolworths, Promenade
21. Sands Venue Resort Hotel and Showtown Museum, Promenade
22. Lifeboat Station, Promenade
23. Sandcastle Waterpark, Promenade
24. Tram Depot at Starr Gate
25. Town Hall, Talbot Square
26. Central Library and Grundy Art Gallery, Queen Street
27. Victoria Hospital, Whinney Heys Road
28. Fire Station, No. 62 Forest Gate
29. Moor Park Health and Leisure Centre, Bristol Avenue
30. Police HQ, Gerry Richardson Way, Marton
31. Blackpool and The Fylde College
32. Bispham Parish Church and Sundial, All Hallows Road
33. Water Tower, Leys Road
34. Savoy Garage, No. 2 King Edward Avenue
35. Queens Park Redevelopment, Layton
36. Blackpool North Station, Talbot Road
37. Funny Girls (former Odeon Cinema), Dickson Road
38. General Post Office (GPO) and its 8 'K6' telephone boxes, Nos 26–30 Abingdon Street
39. Abingdon Street Market
40. St John's Church, St John's Square, Church Street
41. Houndshill Shopping Centre
42. Raikes Hall, Liverpool Road
43. Grange Park
44. Blackpool Zoo, East Park Drive
45. Revoe Library and Gymnasium, Central Drive
46. Blackpool Football Club, Bloomfield Road
47. Saddle Inn, No. 286 Whitegate Drive, Marton
48. Marton Institute, Oxford Square
49. Little Marton Mill, Preston New Road
50. The Cottage at Blowing Sands, No. 166 Common Edge Road, Marton Moss

Introduction

Change in Blackpool is the norm. Whilst most of Blackpool's prominent buildings are well established and intimately associated with entertainment or the tourism industry, there has been a substantial amount of public sector development in recent years and several impressive buildings built.

    This book consists of photographs and details of fifty of Blackpool's most well-known buildings and the authors have tried to include buildings from all areas of the town. At this time, Blackpool has one Grade I listed building, six Grade II*

Regent Cinema, Church Street, Grade II listed.

listed buildings, forty Grade II listed buildings and over 280 buildings listed by the council as being of local interest. To ensure a degree of diversity in the book we have not included all of the listed buildings. Instead links to relevant websites are provided in the section 'Sources and Acknowledgements' at the end of the book.

It would have been tempting to include some of the buildings that are fondly remembered but have been 'lost' from the landscape (Derby Baths/The Palace/ Lewis's/Central station to name a few). We hope readers will look at our 2019 book titled *Lost Blackpool* for photographs and information on such places, and similarly, our (2016) book titled *Blackpool Pubs*, which includes photographs and details of many of the pubs in the town that have closed or been demolished over the years.

The book starts with what we consider to be the eight most prominent buildings or topics, namely the Tower and Tower Building, the Winter Gardens and Opera House, the Three Piers, the Golden Mile, Stanley Park, the Pleasure Beach, the Talbot Gateway buildings and the new sea walls. We then look at Grade II* listed buildings, buildings on the Promenade, followed by public buildings and end with other buildings around Blackpool.

The book has been put together largely through the Covid-19 period of 2020–21 and, as a result, some of the photographs show people wearing face masks.

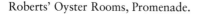

Roberts' Oyster Rooms, Promenade.

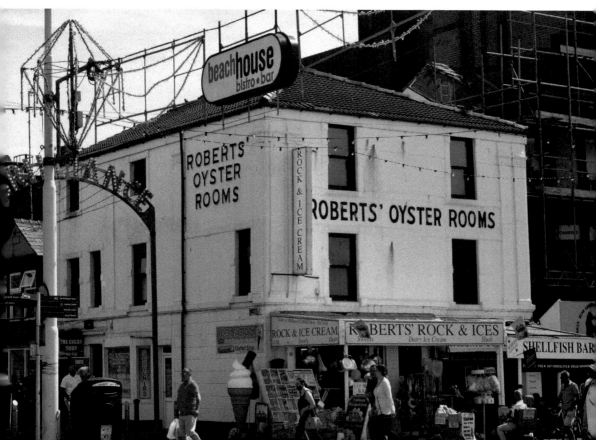

Blackpool's Most Prominent Buildings

1. Blackpool Tower

Blackpool Tower is Blackpool's sole Grade 1 listed building. The listed parts of the building include the Tower itself, the ballroom, circus and roof gardens. The Tower was inspired by Eiffel Tower in Paris, which opened in 1889. The Tower was constructed for the Blackpool Tower Company. The former mayor, Sir John Bickerstaffe, was appointed as chairman of the new company and he was the driving force by ensuring the completion and opening of the Tower to the public on 14 May 1894. It was designed by architects James Maxwell and Charles Tuke and constructed by contractors Heenan & Froude of Manchester. It costs approximately £290,000 to design and build the Tower and Tower Buildings.

Below left: Blackpool Tower, Promenade.

Below right: Tower at night from the air. (Gregg Wolstenholme)

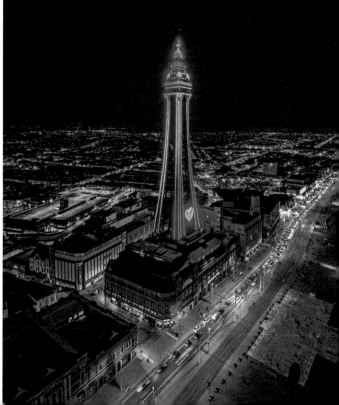

Above: Tower Ballroom. (Michael D. Beckwith)

Left: Tower Circus. (Historic England)

Construction of the foundations for the Tower started in 1891, with erection of the steelworks commencing in March 1892. It is calculated some 2,493 tons of steel and 93 tons of cast iron were used to build the structure, along with 5 million Accrington bricks. It is 480 feet (146 metres) to the crow's nest and 518 feet 9 inches (158 metres) to the top of the flag staff. It has two lifts from the ground floor to the floor at the 55-foot level. From there, the lifts ascend 325 feet to the Blackpool Tower Eye.

The Tower Ballroom was designed by Frank Matcham in the lavish style of the Paris Opera House and opened in August 1899, replacing the original Tower Pavilion. The ballroom floor is 120 feet × 102 feet (37 metres × 31 metres) and is made up of 30,602 blocks of mahogany, oak and walnut. Above the stage is the inscription 'Bid me discourse, I will enchant thine ear', from the poem 'Venus and Adonis' by William Shakespeare. The ballroom was damaged by fire in December 1956 and the dance floor was destroyed, along with the restaurant underneath. The ballroom's plasterwork was restored to its original form by Andrew Mazzei at a cost of £500,000 and the restaurant then became the Tower Lounge. The BBC series *Come Dancing* was televised from the Tower Ballroom for many years and the ballroom now regularly hosts editions of the BBC's *Strictly Come Dancing*. The ballroom is also noted for its Wurlitzer organ, made famous by its resident organist, Reginald Dixon ('Mr Blackpool') in the period 1930 until his retirement in 1970. The Tower Lounge Bar was a large pub accessed from Bank Hey Street and the Promenade, with a capacity of 1,700. It closed in 2014 and is now predominantly the site of a Harry Ramsden's fish and chip restaurant.

Right: Front elevation drawing of the Tower. (Institution of Civil Engineers)

Below: Drone view of the Tower. (Mark Spencer)

THE BLACKPOOL TOWER.
MESSRS. MAXWELL AND TUKE, ARCHITECTS, MANCHESTER.
(For Description, see Page 343.)

Fig. 1.

The Tower Circus is housed underneath the arched girders of the four main legs. The circus opened on 14 May 1894, when admission was from 6*d* (equivalent to 2.5p today), and the circus has not missed a season since. The circus ring can be lowered and filled with 42,000 gallons (190,000 litres) of water at a depth of up to 4 feet 6 inches (1.37 metres), which allows for Grand Finales with Dancing Fountains. The red-nosed clown, Charlie Cairoli, appeared at the circus between 1939 and 1979. The excellent Mooky and his brother Mr Boo are now the resident clowns at the circus. Animals appeared in the circus until 1990 and it was not uncommon to see elephants or horses exercising on the beach opposite the Tower in the early morning. The Tower menagerie (zoo) continued operating until 1973 when it was closed following the opening of Blackpool Zoo, near Stanley Park. The aquarium closed in 2010 and the fish were relocated in the nearby Sea Life Centre.

The Tower was owned by the Bickerstaffe family until 1964, when it was sold to EMI. The Tower complex was renamed Tower World in 1992 and was opened by Diana, Princess of Wales. The Tower itself was painted gold in its centenary year (1994). In 1998, a 'Walk of Faith' glass floor panel was opened at the top of the Tower. Blackpool Council bought Blackpool Tower in 2010 and has subsequently undertaken substantial external structural repairs. The Merlin Entertainment Group now manages the Tower complex and has added various attractions. These include a new Dungeon attraction in the location of the aquarium and a rebranded observation deck at the top of the Tower called the Blackpool Tower Eye.

2. The Winter Gardens and Opera House, Church Street

The rapid development of Blackpool as a holiday location, the increasing numbers of visitors, the variable weather and the desire to create an indoor (all-year round) entertainment facility surpassing anything elsewhere in the country led to the establishment of the Winter Gardens Company in 1875. The site chosen for the Winter Gardens was the Bank Hey estate of Dr W. H. Cocker, at the top of Victoria Street. Part of the house remains within the Winter Gardens. Whilst construction of the Church Street entrance, with its 120-feet-high circular glass dome, the Grand Pavilion, Vestibule and the elegant Floral Hall was underway, an open-air roller-skating rink opened on the site on 27 July 1876 and an indoor skating rink was completed in 1877. The official opening of the Winter Gardens was on 11 July 1878.

The Empress Ballroom, designed by Mangnall and Littlewood, and the Indian Lounge both date from 1896 to 1897. A glass arch at the Coronation Street entrance was completed in 1897. The 220-foot Great Wheel opened in 1896 on the Coronation Street/Adelaide Street corner of the site but closed in 1928 and was dismantled in 1929. In 1930, when the Olympia was built, the bold Winter Gardens arch facing the sea at the top of Victoria Street and the Coronation

Right: Coronation Street entrance.

Below: Church Street entrance.

Street elevation was clad in white faience. The Winter Gardens was acquired by the Tower Company on 9 February 1928 and the Spanish Hall opened in 1931, created on a mezzanine floor in the Coronation Street Palm House area. In the corners of the Spanish Hall, the designer Andrew Mazzei included representations of an Andalusian village.

For many years the Winter Gardens hosted the annual conferences for the main British political parties. The newly completed conference and exhibition centre on Leopold Grove is aimed at resurrecting the Winter Gardens as a premier events venue. The Winter Gardens and Empress Ballroom have been the home of the Blackpool Dance Festival since 1920, an international event with competitors entering from over fifty countries. It has hosted the World Matchplay Darts Tournament since 1994 and also, since 1978, the Blackpool Pigeon Show (The Royal Pigeon Racing Association Show of the Year). EMI took over the Tower Company (and the Winter Gardens) in 1968 and First Leisure took over in 1983. Leisure Parcs Ltd acquired the Winter Gardens in 1998 and the Winter Gardens were purchased by Blackpool Council in 2010. The Winter Gardens is a Grade II* listed building.

The original Her Majesty's Opera House on Church Street, designed by Frank Matcham, opened on 10 June 1889 and was rebuilt in 1910–11, with a new façade in a Renaissance style and clad with white faience. The Opera House we know today opened on 14 July 1939 and was designed by Charles McKeith in an art deco style. The theatre staged the first Royal Command Variety Performance outside of London on 13 April 1955 in front of Her Majesty the Queen and the late HRH the Duke of Edinburgh. It also staged the 81st Royal Variety Performance in the presence of Her Majesty the Queen on 7 December 2009, which was compered by Peter Kay. On 29 November 2020, the Opera House hosted a 'virtual' Royal Variety Performance, compered by Jason Manford with a special message from HRH The Prince of Wales.

Dome of the
Winter Garden.

Above: Floral Hall. (Michael D. Beckwith)

Below: Empresss Ballroom. (Michael D. Beckwith)

Above: Opera House Theatre. (Blackpool Entertainment Company Limited)

Below: Spanish Hall. (Michael D. Beckwith)

3. The Three Piers

Uniquely in the UK, Blackpool has three piers. Blackpool's first pier, the Grade II listed North Pier, was designed by Eugenius Birch and is the oldest surviving example of his piers still in use. North Pier opened on 21 May 1863 and 20,000 people attended the opening ceremony, which included a cannon salute, procession and civic reception. It was built by Richard Laidlow & Son at a cost of £11,740 and was originally 468 yards (428 metres) long and 9 yards (8.2 metres) wide, widening to 18 yards (16 metres) at the pier head. It stands on cast-iron screw piles with a wooden deck. There were 275,000 admissions in the first year, 400,000 in the second year and 465,000 in the third year. The pier head was extended to accommodate the Indian Pavilion, which opened in 1877. The Indian Pavilion was destroyed by fire in 1921, rebuilt and again burnt down in 1938 and was replaced by a 1,564-seat theatre in 1939. The end of pier theatre has hosted many stars and has been renamed the Joe Longthorne Theatre after the singer who performed there for twenty seasons from 1987. The 158-yard- (144-metre-) long jetty was built between 1868 and 1869. The jetty facilitated the operation of paddle steamers in its early days and later sea angling. It was cut off from the pier following storms in December 1997 and demolished around 2000. The Sun Lounge at the south end of the pier was the home of resident Wurlitzer organist Raymond Wallbank between 1963 and 1995. Sooty, the mischievous yellow bear

North Pier.

Above: View of North Pier from just to the south.

Below: Along North Pier.

hand puppet, was bought by magician and entertainer Harry Corbett in 1948 from a stall on North Pier. Harry and Sooty became famous from the late 1950s through children's TV. The Merry England Bar and an amusement arcade were added in the 1960s. A Victorian-style entrance was created in the 1980s and 1991 saw the addition of a small tramway along the pier and the Carousel Bar. Other attractions on the pier include an ice cream parlour, a palm reader and a beautiful carousel. In 2004, North Pier was voted Pier of the Year by the National Piers Society. It was bought by the Sedgwick family in 2011.

Central Pier is Blackpool's second pier and was originally known as South Pier. It was designed by Lieutenant-Colonel John Isaac Mawson and opened on 30 May 1868. It was also built by Laidlaw & Son of Glasgow. The pier was originally 503 yards long (460 metres), including a jetty of 131 yards (120 metres) when it opened. Paddle steamers such as the *Queen of the North* and the *Bickerstaffe* sailed from Central Pier on day trips to Morecambe, Llandudno and other places. Central Pier became known as 'The People's Pier' because it appealed to the working-class holidaymakers with the provision of entertainment centred

Central Pier.

around dancing and having fun. Roller skating, fairground rides and amusement machines were introduced in the early twentieth century. Later in the century, bars and a theatre were opened. The Dixieland Showbar opened in 1968 and was destroyed by fire in 1973. The theatre was modernised in 1986 and was renamed Maggie May's Showbar, with Linda Nolan playing there for nine seasons. It later became Peggy Sue's Showboat and then Legends. In 1990, the 108-foot (33-metre) Ferris Wheel was installed, which necessitated the strengthening of the structure to cope with the extra weight. Both Central and South Piers were bought by the Sedgwick family in July 2015.

South Pier was known as Victoria Pier until 1930. It was designed by T. P. Worthington and built at a cost of £50,000. The pier opened on Good Friday 1893, with the 3,000-seat capacity Grand Pavilion opening on 20 May 1893. The pier is 164 yards (149 metres) long. It is shorter than the other two piers but was built wider to accommodate pavilions. It also had a bandstand, thirty-six shops, a photographic studio and an ice cream vendor. The pier head theatre was demolished in 1998 to make way for the Crazy Mouse roller coaster. Today's other attractions include Pirates Bay Family Bar, funfair, Old Time Portrait Studio, game stalls, cafés, kiddies rides, the Skycoaster 124-foot (38-metre) freefalling swing, Skyscreamer reverse bungee ride, Spider Mountain climbing web, Maxibounce safety harnessed trampoline, stalls, cafés, kiosks and the Laughing Donkey Family Bar, which has live entertainment.

Aerial view of Central Pier. (Gregg Wolstenholme)

Right: South Pier.

Below: South Pier at night. (Gregg Wolstenholme)

4. The Golden Mile

There are differing opinions as to where the 'Golden Mile' starts and finishes along the Promenade. The authors' view is that it runs the length of the Promenade from south of what was the Palatine Hotel at Hounds Hill (now the site of the new Sands Resort Venue Hotel) to Central Pier. This popular length of promenade was originally known as 'South Beach'. As Blackpool became more accessible and popular in the mid to late 1800s, boarding houses, hotels and pubs were built along the promenade to cater for visitors. Both North Pier and Central station opened in 1863 and Central Pier (then known as South Pier) opened in 1868. The Tower opened in 1894 and Blackpool was booming. Due to its proximity to the town's main tourist attractions and the easy (almost level) natural access to the beach, this central beach area was a haven for all kinds of people selling ice cream, drinks, oysters, as well as boatmen, donkey rides, Punch and Judy shows, quack doctors, palmists and fancy goods dealers. On 2 March 1897, the council banned certain classes of activities from the beach and the excluded traders simply negotiated with the owners of the houses opposite (along 'South Beach') and started trading from their gardens. The gardens soon became forecourts and then the properties themselves were gradually taken over and became amusement arcades. Today, all the original properties have gone and the Golden Mile is dominated by larger developments including Coral Island, the Golden Mile Amusements building, the Sea Life Centre, Funland and Madame Tussauds.

Golden Mile from Central Pier.

Above: Coral Island, Golden Mile.

Below: Golden Mile Amusements.

Golden Mile at night.

5. Stanley Park

Alderman Sir Albert Lindsay Parkinson was fundamental in securing the land for Stanley Park in 1920, which allowed Blackpool Corporation to commission landscape architects T. H. Mawson & Sons to prepare plans for the park and recreational facilities. It was officially opened on 2 October 1926 by Lord Derby. Mawson's ambitious design transformed an area of dilapidated buildings, pigsties, stagnant ponds and a brickworks into a park that was voted the best park in the UK (2017 and 2019) by Fields in Trust. Stanley Park is Grade II* listed and is on the Register of Historic Parks and Gardens of special historic interest in England. The main entrance to the park is through the splendid iron gates at the start of the Mawson Drive 'boulevard', leading to the car park adjacent to the art deco-style café building and terrace, designed by J. C. Robinson, which opened in 1937. The centrepiece and 'heart' of Stanley Park is the circular Italian Gardens with its marble fountain, paths, and geometrical beds, usually adorned in swathes of colour. South of the Italian Gardens is the 26-metre-high clock tower memorial to Dr William Henry Cocker, Blackpool's first mayor. It was designed in 1926 and built in Portland stone. It closed to the public in the mid-1970s. The park also features a 26-acre boating lake, boathouses, a bandstand with seating for 2,500 in its semicircular amphitheatre, tennis courts, athletics ground (track upgraded in 1987) with a stand seating 300 spectators, putting courses, six bowling greens, playing fields, sunken oval-shaped rose garden and an eighteen-hole golf course designed by Dr Alister MacKenzie. The clubhouse was built in 1935. Within the

Above: Italian Gardens.

Below: Stanley Park Lake.

Opposite: Cocker Tower.

Above: Café building and fountain.

Right: Bandstand.

park area and adjacent to West Park Drive is the 5,000-seat Blackpool Cricket Club. To the eastside of the park is the Model Village, which opened in 1972. In recent years, further recreational facilities have been added to the park area including all-weather sports pitches (1987 and 2008), an indoor sports centre (1996), Visitor's Centre (2005), a children's playground, the High Ropes Course, a national BMX racetrack (2011) and a skate park. Construction work started on the former tearoom and tennis pavilion in March 2022 to transform it into a new refreshment facility and changing rooms for local youth clubs.

6. The Pleasure Beach

The multi-award-winning Pleasure Beach amusement park began as an informal fairground in the 1890s on the sand dunes area of the Watson Estate, South Shore, south of Balmoral Road. In 1903, in conjunction with local businessman John Outhwaite, William George Bean bought 30 acres of the estate and developed it as the Pleasure Beach. Rides such as Sir Hiram Maxim's Captive Flying Machine (1904), River Caves of the World (1905), the Scenic Railway (1907; the park's first wooden rollercoaster), and the Big Dipper (1923) were introduced. Bean died of pneumonia in 1929 and left the fairground to his daughter Doris, whose husband Leonard Thompson took over the running and development of the park for the next forty-seven years, until his death in 1976. Doris Thompson became chairman, and their son Geoffrey Thompson OBE became managing director. Following Geoffrey's death in 2004, Geoffrey's daughter Amanda Thompson OBE took over the running of the business. The park has ten roller coasters, including the Big Dipper; Grand National; Avalanche (bobsled ride); the Big One, which at 62 metres is the tallest in the UK; and Icon, the newest roller coaster, which opened in May 2018. Six acres of the site is now Nickleodeon Land, which opened in May 2011, a children's theme park with rides including SpongeBob's Splash Bash, Nickelodeon Streak roller coaster and Rugrats Lost River ride. The Pleasure Beach Arena is an indoor ice rink where professional ice skaters perform

White Tower Casino, Pleasure Beach.

Above: Sir Hiram Maxim's Captive Flying Machine. (Blackpool Pleasure Beach)

Right: Big Dipper. (Blackpool Pleasure Beach)

Revolution. (Blackpool Pleasure Beach)

Above: The Big One.

Below: Icon. (Blackpool Pleasure Beach)

the world-renowned Hot Ice Show produced by Amanda Thompson. It has been running since 1937 and seats some 2,000 spectators. The art deco Casino at the north-west corner of the park was built in 1937–40 to the design of Joseph Emberton. Today the building performs a number of roles including main ticket office, a Costa Coffee café, the Horseshoe Show Bar, the Paradise Room function suite, the Attic Moroccan-themed function room and White Tower restaurant. In the basement is the Pasaje del Terror horror maze and the Horror Bar. The Pleasure Beach is served by two on-site hotels, the four-star Big Blue Hotel (opened in 2003) next to which is the 120-room Boulevard Hotel, built in 2019 on the site of the former Star pub.

7. Talbot Gateway, Talbot Road

The Talbot Gateway is a redevelopment scheme that has transformed the area to the east of the town centre and adjacent to Blackpool North station. Since 2009, Blackpool Council and Muse Developments have been working together to develop the Central Business District. Phase 1 of the scheme began in 2012 with the clearance of buildings between Cookson Street and Buchanan Street, including the Indoor Bowling Centre, followed by the construction of Bickerstaffe House, the redevelopment of Talbot Road bus station and car park and the building of the new Sainsbury's supermarket. Bickerstaffe House, at No. 1 Bickerstaffe Square, is a five-storey glass fronted building and has retail units at ground floor, a central courtyard, and now houses Blackpool Council staff offices. It was designed by Aedas Architects (now AHR). It was built by Eric Wright Construction Ltd and completed in 2014. It is named after Sir John Bickerstaffe JP, former mayor and chairman of the Tower Company until his death on 5 August 1930, at the age of eighty-two.

Talbot Gateway – Phase 1 at night.

Above: Bickerstaffe House, Talbot Road.

Below: Sainsbury's, Talbot Road.

Talbot Road car park.

Talbot Road car park was the first true municipal multistorey car park in Britain. It has a steel and concrete frame and was built by Atherton Bros Ltd between 1937 and 1939 to a design by G. W. Stead, an engineer at Blackpool Corporation. The cavernous ground floor was open and the ceiling height was designed to accommodate double-decker buses, which came in at the rear Cookson Street corner and left by the Talbot Road frontage. The car park on the four upper floors and roof provided space for 750 cars. There was a basement housing public toilets. Its original cream and green exterior (the colours of the Corporation buses and trams for many years) displayed coloured panels depicting progress in transport. The building was re-clad in the 1960s as the tiles were unsafe. The building was initially earmarked for demolition in 2006 but the car park has been refurbished and tastefully clad with translucent material. The ground floor area that was the bus station is now occupied by 'The Gym' and Mr Basrai's World Cuisines.

The new 120,000-square-feet Sainsbury's superstore on Talbot Road is a three-storey building with 58,000 square feet of retail space, a café, a Timpson's shoe repair shop and an Argos outlet. It was built by Shepherd Construction and Barr Construction. The curved glass-fronted store has six zigzag travelators and a 600-space car park. The project architect was Leach Rhodes Walker. The new store opened on 23 July 2014.

8. The Sea Walls

The main geological features of Blackpool along the seafront are the sand/upper boulder clay cliffs to the northern half of the town and the low-lying sandy (and sometimes peaty) land to the south. The cliffs essentially start just south of the Tower and rise to a height of about 80 feet (over 24 metres) north of the Gynn before the land drops down to sea level at Anchorsholme. There are reports from 1936 that erosion to the cliffs had been estimated to be 2 yards per annum in the previous thirty years. To the south, due to the low-lying nature of the land, flooding of the seafront land and properties on spring tides was not uncommon.

As Blackpool started to develop as a tourist destination from the mid-1700s and properties were built along the seafront, attempts to halt erosion and flooding were made by the building of ad hoc sea defences. From the mid-1850s, the local authority began to construct more substantial sea defence works. Between 1865 and 1870 a new promenade from Cocker Square to South Shore, near to where South Pier is today, was constructed using granite setts laid on puddled clay to a slope of 1 in 4, topped with three rows of wooden sleepers fixed perpendicular to the slope. Originally the Claremont Estate Company, who owned the land between Cocker Square and the Gynn, stone-pitched the lower part of the cliffs along that length in 1876. Between 1895 and 1899, the Corporation constructed

Cocker Square to Gynn Square.

a new sea wall along this length (the North Shore Works) at a cost of £150,000, using pink granite blocks for the sloping apron and a curved upper concrete wall.

Between 1902 and 1905 the Promenade between North and South Piers was widened by 100 feet. Sand was taken from the low water line by horse and cart, largely using men with shovels. The sea wall that was in front of the Tower until recently was faced with black basalt blocks from the Rhine. From 1910 and following the extension of Blackpool's boundary from just north of the Gynn to Cleveleys, sea walls were constructed in a northerly direction, with completion to the northern boundary in 1936. Princess Parade was constructed in 1910–11 with the walls faced with basalt pitching imported from the Giant's Causeway and the sand infill taken from South Shore and transported on train lines along the Promenade by the 'Sands Express' (*Annie, Horbury, Netherton, Reliance* and *Alice* – engines). Between 1922 and 1926, the sea wall from South Pier to Starr Gate was constructed and the sea wall extended 400 feet west of the old beach. In 1923, South Shore Open Air Baths opened. Following the storms of 1977 and the damage caused to the ageing structures, a twenty-year plan was developed to renew and strengthen the existing sea walls. The first scheme to be completed in 1982 was the length between Cocker Square and the Gynn, followed by the length between the Gynn and the north side of the Boating Pool.

In 1995, the council adopted a detailed Shoreline Protection Strategy to ensure the stability of the sea walls and their continuing maintenance. The sea wall at

Looking south from North Pier.

Above: Looking north from South Pier.

Below: Sea wall, South Promenade. (D. Thorley-Pixabay)

New South Promenade, south of the Sandcastle to the southern boundary at Starr Gate, was undertaken in three phases and completed in 2001. The sea defences along this length incorporate hexagonal concrete units (known as 'Sea Bee' units) that are similar in shape to the nut, from a nut and bolt, and help dissipate the energy of the waves when they crash against them. Along this 2-km length a trail of public artwork now comprising eight pieces of unique art, including the Mirror Ball. The sea defences between Cocker Square and the Sandcastle (some 3.2 km) were renewed and improved over a four-year period ending in 2009 at a cost of £62 million. Five curved 'headlands' extending into the sea were built. The Tower Headland is the northernmost headland and includes the 'Comedy Carpet' typographic artwork, which opened in October 2011. The area is able to hold 20,000 spectators in outdoor events. Buff-coloured precast concrete was used for the sea wall and stepped aprons to match the colour of the sand on the beach. The £27-million Anchorsholme Coast Protection Scheme from Little Bispham to the town's northern boundary at Anchorsholme was constructed over a two and a half year period by Balfour Beatty and was officially opened on Monday 30 October 2017. The sea wall provides flood protection to the surrounding community and the project has improved the road and access to Anchorsholme Park.

Mirror Ball and Shelter.

Grade II* Listed Buildings

A cenotaph is an empty tomb and reminds us that not all bodies of the fallen are repatriated from war zones. In 1918, a temporary war shrine was built on Princess Parade in the sunken garden to the south of the Metropole Hotel and was replaced in 1919 by another temporary shrine. In 1923 the magnificent Grade II* listed structure we know today was erected. It was designed by Ernest Prestwich and built by H. A. Clegg & Sons. The 30-metre-tall Cornish granite obelisk (the tallest war memorial in England) sits on a square plinth. Around the base of the

Blackpool War Memorial (Cenotaph), Princess Parade.

'Lest We Forget', Blackpool
War Memorial (Cenotaph).

structure are bronze relief sculptures by Gilbert Ledward. These are regarded as
unusual because the plaques include the depiction of women. It includes a nurse, a
wife and child left behind, a grieving widow and daughter and even more unusual
is the depiction of a fallen German soldier. The war memorial was restored in
2007–08 when the stonework and bronzes were cleaned. A new memorial, the
'Choir Loft', designed by Ruth Barker, was unveiled on 27 June 2008 by the
Duchess of Cornwall and dedicated to civilian casualties.

1c. The Church of the Sacred Heart, No. 17 Talbot Road

The Roman Catholic Church of the Sacred Heart, on Talbot Road, was
Blackpool's first Roman Catholic Church. The western part of the present church
opened on 8 December 1857. It was built in an English Gothic style to a design
by architect Edward Pugin and was originally dedicated to 'The Sacred Hearts of
Jesus and Mary'. Miss Monica Tempest of Broughton Hall near Skipton paid for
the building of the church on the condition that it must be served by the Society
of Jesus. In the 1890s the church was enlarged to a design by Edward's brother,
Peter Paul Pugin. The original high altar and Lady Chapel were moved eastwards
and the large octagonal extension built, with its 109-foot (33-metre) tower and
lantern of brick, with stone cladding. It reopened in 1894. The tower has four
stages, angled buttresses and corner pinnacles. Its plan consists of a four-bay nave
with an octagonal crossing around which the aisles and transept lie. Above the
crossing is an octagonal pyramidal slate roof, above which is an octagonal lantern
with pyramidal copper clad roof. The former school, to the west, was built in
1898 and is now the Little Black Pug Café/Bar. To the east is the neo-Georgian

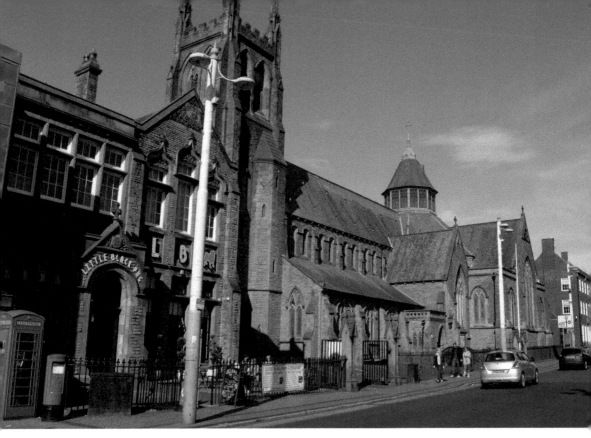

Above: The Church of the Sacred Heart, No. 17 Talbot Road.

Below: The semicircular sanctuary of the Church of the Sacred Heart.

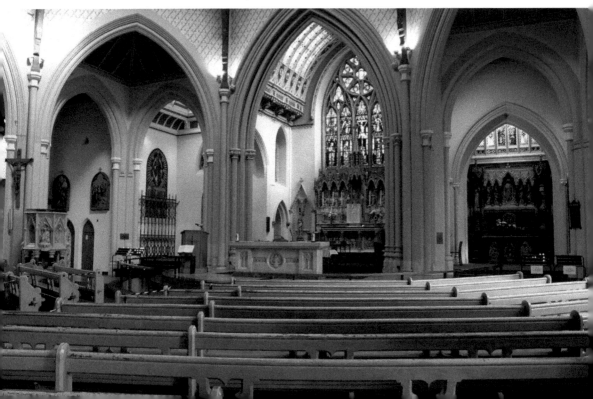

presbytery built around 1950. Interestingly there is an organ in the west gallery with fine panelling of American mahogany. The organ was purchased by the parish priest Fr Oldham from the Waterloo cinema in 1935. The semicircular sanctuary was constructed in 1972 and the side altar at St Joseph's shrine was installed as the new high altar, facing the congregation. The benches under the lantern were rearranged around the sanctuary to involve the congregation more closely in the liturgical action. On 18 April 2004 the Jesuits left, and the church is now served by Lancaster diocese. Mass is held three times on Sunday and once on all other days. Also, vigil mass is held on Saturday with Sacrament of Reconciliation on Friday and Saturday. The church is open every day from 8 a.m. until late, allowing people of any faith or no faith to pray or have a quiet moment.

11. Grand Theatre, No. 33 Church Street

The Grand Theatre opened on the corner of Church Street and Corporation Street (previously St Ann Street) on 23 July 1894. It was designed by the famous theatre architect Frank Matcham and built for theatre manager Thomas Sergenson at a cost £20,000. The three-storey corner entrance is in a baroque style with a domed roof of copper fish-scale tiles, topped by a cupola. Inside the theatre the

Grand Theatre, No. 33 Church Street.

Grand Theatre stage. (Michael D. Beckwith)

auditorium has 1,153 blue velvet seats and three 'cantilevered' balconies. The interior of the theatre is richly decorated with gilding, painted wall and ceiling panels and plaster decoration. Sergenson sold the theatre to the Blackpool Tower Company in 1909. The theatre thrived in its early years as a summer season venue. Gracie Fields made all her Blackpool Variety appearances at the Grand between 1932 and 1938. Later, the theatre suffered due to competition from cinemas and the rise in popularity of television. The Grand was granted Grade II* listing on 26 January 1972. Later, plans to demolish the theatre were successfully resisted by the Friends of the Grand and the local authority. After a period when the theatre was not used and a further period when it was used as a bingo hall, the owners (EMI) agreed to lease and eventually sell the theatre to the Blackpool Grand Theatre Trust Ltd on 1 October 1980. The Grand reopened as a theatre on 23 March 1981 and in May 1981 the theatre hosted a Royal Variety Performance in the presence of Prince Charles, the Prince of Wales. Extensive restoration work was begun in the early 1990s, which was completed in 2007. On Tuesday 23 July 2019, the Grand Theatre celebrated its 125th anniversary. Despite the ravages of the Covid-19 pandemic and whilst relying heavily on grants, donations and sponsorship, the theatre strives to provide a wide and varied programme.

12. The Shrine of Our Lady of Lourdes, Whinney Heys Road

During the Second World War the Diocese of Lancaster suffered relatively little bombing compared to many other parts of the country. The Right Reverend Thomas Flynn, Bishop of Lancaster, conceived the idea for the shrine as an offering to God to show gratitude for the diocese being spared. William Eaves gifted the land for the church and also gifted the land on the other side of the road to ensure the shrine would have an open aspect. The £50,000 building cost was funded by every parish in the diocese. The shrine was designed by Francis Xavier Veldarde and built by Eaves & Co. It opened on 30 June 1957, having taken two years to build. It was built using Portland stone under a copper clad roof. David John sculptured the pinnacles on each corner representing Our Lady appearing to St Bernadette, Christ appearing to St Margaret Mary, St Thomas of Canterbury and St Edward the Confessor. He also sculpted the relief frieze of the Holy Trinity above the front door. The interior is equally impressive with gold mosaic, brightly coloured paints and marble. The shrine was deconsecrated in 1993. The building became a Grade II* listed building in 1999, with ownership transferring to the Historic Chapels Trust in 2000. English Heritage granted £80,000 for urgent repairs, which were completed in 2008. The Historic Chapels Trust is raising funds for further renovations after which the chapel will be made available to the community for events such as exhibitions, concerts and occasional religious services.

Below left: The Shrine of Our Lady of Lourdes, Whinney Heys Road.

Below right: Relief frieze-front door, the Shrine of Our Lady of Lourdes.

Buildings on the Promenade

Norbreck Villa was built at the end of the eighteenth century as a privately owned country house and was purchased by James Shorrocks around 1900, who held lavish parties there. In 1912 he formed a public company and launched an expansion program to turn the house into a hotel named Norbreck Hall Hydro. The next two decades saw the addition of a ballroom, swimming pool and solarium, patronised by the nobility and upper classes. The hotel was commandeered during the Second World War for use as offices and accommodation for evacuated civil servants. The building was handed back in 1951 and at that time had an eighteen-hole golf course, bowling green and tennis courts on the promenade frontage, 400 bedrooms and a 600-seat restaurant. From the 1970s the hotel became the venue for a number of music concerts including Adam and the Ants, The Pretenders, Def Leppard, Iron Maiden, Stray Cats and Ozzy Osborne's first solo appearance after leaving Black Sabbath. The Liberal Party and the Social Democratic Party held a conference at the hotel in 1988 where they merged and became the Liberal Democrats (Lib Dems). Today,

Norbreck Castle Hotel, Queen's Promenade.

the Norbreck Castle Hotel is owned by Britannia Hotels and has 480 bedrooms and twenty-two conference suites (including the Norcalympia, which can hold 3,000 delegates). Events at the hotel include world-class indoor bowling tournaments, Europe's biggest Elvis Presley competition/convention and the UK's largest model boat show, held every October.

14. Miners' Convalescent Home, Queen's Promenade

The former Miners' Convalescent Home on Queen's Promenade at Bispham is a Grade II listed building and was built between 1925 and 1927 as a convalescent home for Lancashire and Cheshire miners. It was designed by architects Bradshaw Gass & Hope in the baroque revival style and was opened by Edward, Prince of Wales, in 1927. It has four storeys (including attic) and has a symmetrical frontage built in red and light-coloured engineering brick with terracotta dressings under a hipped slate roof. The facilities included a reading room, billiard room, smoke room, concert hall (with cinema), recreation room, winter garden, and accommodation for some 125 patients. Outdoors were gardens and to the front were two bowling greens. It is said that patients were often wheeled out whilst still in their beds to enjoy the sea air. The funds to pay for the home came from the Miners' Welfare Levy, which was a national levy of 1*d* per ton of all coal produced. The home operated until 1987 and was converted into apartments in 1995. It then became known as Admiral Point at which time two new apartment blocks known as Admiral View and Admiral Heights were built in the grounds along with new housing to the rear of the site.

Miners' Convalescent Home, Queen's Promenade.

15. Shelters on the Promenade

There are sixteen historic shelters on the promenade, west of the tramway, ten of which are on the clifftop between Wolverton Avenue and Little Bispham. The shelters are Grade II listed and are thought to have been built around 1904. The three pairs of Grade II listed shelters that were originally to the west of the tramway

Left: Shelters on Queen's Promenade.

Below: Shelters on Princess Parade.

opposite Alexandra Road, Wellington Road and Trafalgar Road, flanking steps to the beach at each location, were relocated to Princess Parade in 2011 when the new promenade works were undertaken at South Shore. The shelters generally have ornamental brackets in an open arabesque pattern originally supporting a lead-covered swept out pavilion-shaped roof with blind bullseye dormers in each side and a needle-shaped iron finial in the centre of the roof. The shelters are painted in a classic green colour.

16. Cabin Lift at the Boating Pool, Queen's Promenade

Sometimes known as the Boating Pool lift, the Cabin Lift gets its name from the former Uncle Tom's Cabin pub, which was on the edge of the cliffs, west of the tram tracks. The Cabin Lift is a Grade II listed building and is unusual in that it originally incorporated public toilets and a tram shelter. The building was designed by the Borough Surveyor J. C. Robinson in a similar style to other Robinson designs of public buildings in Blackpool, utilising red brickwork, a copper pyramid roof, and decorative eaves faience cornice. It was built to transport holidaymakers

Cabin Lift at the Boating Pool, Queen's Promenade.

from the upper promenade to the Boating Pool below. It had an intermediate access level one storey up from the lower promenade. The lift was accessed on the upper promenade by a short bridge flanked by brick walls. It opened in 1930 and in its first season it carried 120,000 passengers on the upward journey and 38,100 on the downward journey. The lift closed in 1979 and reopened in 1991 for two seasons. The tram shelter was demolished around 1991.

17. The Imperial Hotel, Promenade

The four-storey central block to the Grade II listed Imperial Hotel on North Promenade was designed by Clegg and Knowles of Manchester to a French Renaissance design. The hotel opened in 1867 having cost £22,170. The south wing (1875 by Mangnall and Littlewood) is built in red brick with stone dressings and hipped slate roofs. The later extension to the north (1904 by J. D. Broadbent) is in a free baroque style with stone-coloured terracotta dressings and a large single-storey pavilion projecting forward. During the First World War the hotel was commandeered and used as a convalescence hospital for shellshocked officers. During the Second World War II the hotel was again requisitioned and became the home of the Ministry of Agriculture and Fisheries until it was handed back in 1951. Among the famous people who have stayed at the Imperial are Queen Elizabeth, Charles Dickens, the Beatles, Sir Winston Churchill and several other prime ministers and political leaders when the main party political conferences were held

Imperial Hotel, Promenade.

The Imperial Hotel's lobby. (Imperial Hotel)

in Blackpool from 1950s to 2007. The Blackpool Civic Trust and The Imperial Hotel were awarded the Blackpool Town Council Conservation Award in 2015 for the restoration work carried out in the hotel's former Turkish baths. The hotel has 180 bedrooms, a ballroom, fourteen function suites, a swimming pool, a games room, Palm Court Restaurant and No. 10 bar (in the former billiard room). Trader Jack's nightclub was established in the lower ground floor/swimming pool area in the 1970s, with DJ Eddie Gee. The space now accommodates a fitness centre. During the 1970s concerts were held in the ballroom with performances from bands such as Joy Division, Judas Priest, AC/DC and Racing Cars.

18. Metropole Hotel, Promenade

Lawrence Bailey, a farmer from Layton, built Bailey's Hotel on a small seafront promontory in the vicinity of Fumblers Hill. It opened around 1785 as one of Blackpool's first hotels and had thirty-four bedrooms, three dining rooms and a coffee lounge. Following his death in 1812, Robert Dickson tenanted the hotel from Bailey's trustees from around 1816 and seems to have bought the hotel in 1827. By 1851, when the hotel was known as Rossall's Dickson Hotel, the hotel was tenanted by John Rossall. Ten years later William Bailey, Dickson's brother-in-law and grandson of Lawrence Bailey, was the licensee and it again became

Metropole Hotel, Promenade.

known as Bailey's Hotel. Later William bought the hotel from Dickson's trustees. In May 1873, the *Gazette* reported the hotel had been pulled down and rebuilt without loss of a season. Shops were added to the eastern elevation in 1876. The hotel was bought by J. T. Murray in 1896, who renamed it Hotel Metropole before selling it to Spiers and Pond Ltd in 1900, when the hotel was further renovated and extended to double its size. The government requisitioned the hotel to be used for the war effort in 1939. F. Price formed a company that bought the hotel in 1947 and sold it to Billy Butlin in 1955, who in turn sold it to Grand Hotels in 1998. The Metropole is now owned by Britannia Hotels and has 223 bedrooms, two restaurants, a café and provides live entertainment. It was, and still is, the only hotel on the seaward side of the Promenade.

19. Festival House, Promenade

One of Blackpool's most interesting new buildings of recent years is Festival House, which was completed in December 2011 on the Promenade, on the west side of the tram tracks, opposite the end of Church Street. This site had housed tourist information offices for many years and this facility has been incorporated into Festival House along with the south facing Beach House Bistro and Bar. On the first floor is a registry office, and above that is the Tower View Room

Above: Festival House, Promenade.

Right: Blackpool Tower reflected by
Festival House.

(a wedding ceremony hall), with its precisely framed view of Blackpool Tower. It was designed by Architect de Rijke Marsh Morgan and built by F. Parkinson Ltd. The award-winning three-storey structure primarily uses prefabricated cross-laminated timber panels manufactured off-site. This is clad in golden stainless steel shingles above a plinth clad in corbelled blocks containing recycled and phosphorescent glass, which glint when they catch the light.

2c. 'Woolworths', Promenade

The site of the iconic Woolworths store on the corner of the Promenade and Adelaide Place was previously occupied primarily by the Royal Hotel and the iron and glass Royal Market. Later a smaller Woolworths store opened (1926) on the north promenade corner of the site adjacent to the Tower and the new flagship store opened in spring 1938. The new store was then Woolworths' largest store and the art deco building was clad in marble cream 'Darwen' glazed blocks and had bright bronze work. The ground floor shop covered the full area of

Above: Woolworths Clock Tower. (Historic England)

Left: Woolworths, Promenade.

the building from the Promenade to Bank Hey Street and there were two large basement sales floors. On the first floor was a large open restaurant seating up to 2,000 with food elevators to the kitchens on the second floor. There was a second, smaller restaurant on the second floor, which was used for parties and as an overflow at busy bank holiday times. There were dishwashing facilities, a cold room, stores and lifts for the shop and restaurant. There was also a bakery on the roof, servicing the café. The square clock tower facing south, with its illuminated 'Woolworths Cafe' sign and flagpole, was a ventilation shaft, pumping cool air into the store. The store closed in September 1984 and opened as Pricebusters from April 1985 to 2008. The building has since been occupied by Wetherspoon's, The Albert and The Lion pub and Poundland on the ground floor and Sports Direct above. The exterior has recently been renovated.

21. Sands Venue Resort Hotel and Showtown Museum, Promenade

Originally, this was the site of a row of houses named Queens Terrace. Following the opening of Central station in 1863, the Palatine Hotel was built on the site opposite the station in the late 1870s and demolished in the 1970s. The site was redeveloped and the Palatine Building erected, with an elevated concrete walkway, which wrapped around the south side of the building, over the tram tracks onto the Promenade. The Palatine Building housed the Sands Venue, which hosted the 'Legends' cabaret show, the Wild West Diner Bar and Grill on the ground floor

Sands Venue Resort Hotel and Showtown Museum, Promenade.

and a restaurant on the first floor. In 2018, Warden Construction Ltd began remodelling the Palatine Building to create the five-star, ninety-one-room Sands Venue Resort Hotel, which is due to open in 2022.

The building will also house Blackpool's museum of fun and entertainment, named Showtown, on the first floor, which is due to open in 2023 at a cost of £13 million. The project has been funded by the Heritage Lottery Fund, the Coastal Communities Fund, the Northern Cultural Fund, the Lancashire Economic Partnership Growth Deal and Blackpool Council. The Showtown museum will have six themes: the seaside, magic, Blackpool shows, the Illuminations, dance and the circus.

22. Lifeboat Station, Promenade

Blackpool's first Royal National Lifeboat Institution lifeboat was the 33-foot *Robert William*, launched on 20 July 1864. It was housed at the Lytham Road lifeboat station just behind the Manchester Hotel. A new lifeboat house, designed by Halstead Best, was opened in 1937 on the Promenade on the north side of Central Pier. In September 1998, the RNLI Blackpool Lifeboat Station and visitor centre opened on the seaward side of the tram tracks on Central Promenade near New Bonny Street. It was built by F. Parkinson Ltd for the RNLI at a cost of

Lifeboat station, Promenade.

£630,000. It is one of only two stations in the country to have three inshore boats. These are the Atlantic 85 lifeboat named *William and Eleanor* (B-867) and the two D class lifeboats named *Basil Eric Brooks* (D-732) and *Eileen Mary George* (D-729). The launch and recovery of the Atlantic Class boat is by tractor and the D Class boats is by Land Rover. The RNLI shop is a charity shop that supports the work of the Royal National Lifeboat Institution and the visitor centre provides local and national information about the RNLI.

23. Sandcastle Waterpark, Promenade

The Sandcastle is the largest indoor water park in the UK. It was built as a public/private joint venture project on the site of the former South Shore Open Air Baths and opened in 1986. The inside temperature is maintained at a tropical 84 degrees and has eighteen slides, including the Masterblaster, which is said to be, at 250 metres, the world's longest indoor rollercoaster waterslide. The northern part of the Sandcastle building previously housed The World of Coronation Street attraction, which included a recreation of the Street and the Rovers Return, as well as set reproductions depicting the history of the programme. The attraction closed and was replaced in August 2001 by a casino, operated by Grosvenor Casinos.

Sandcastle Waterpark, Promenade.

24. Tram Depot at Starr Gate

There are now two tram depots serving Blackpool's trams: one at Rigby Road and the other at Starr Gate. Blackpool's first tram depot opened on Blundell Street in 1885 to serve the conduit car fleet and was enlarged in the 1890s. It could house forty-five trams on five tracks and became a store in 1935 when the larger Rigby Road Depot opened. Rigby Road Depot can house 108 trams. It has maintenance facilities, a tram-washing plant, a paint shop and now houses the heritage trams. The tram depot at Bold Street, Fleetwood, closed in 1920 and depots at Bispham, Marton and Copse Road, Fleetwood, closed in 1963. The Starr Gate Depot has been built on the former car park, tram turning area and go-cart track at Starr Gate. It was built between 2009 and 2011 and officially opened at Easter 2012 as part of the £20 million network refurbishment. The depot building has a sweeping curved roof and three-dimensional wave feature wall panels, which are backlit with LED lights. The depot houses the Flexity 2 fleet of 32-metre long trams, together with maintenance, tram wash and automated sand filling facilities.

Tram depot at Starr Gate.

Public Buildings

25. Blackpool Town Hall, Talbot Square

The Town Hall, in Talbot Square, is a Grade II listed building and was constructed between 1895 and 1900, replacing the earlier Town Hall sited just to the south. The new building cost £81,500 and was designed in a Jacobean style by architects Potts, Son and Hennings. The façades are of Ruabon bricks and Yorkshire stone with a slate roof. Originally, the clock tower had an 180-feet- (55-metre-) high steel and timber spire clad in copper and topped with a ship weather vane, which

Blackpool Town Hall, Talbot Square.

Blackpool Town Hall, Council Chamber. (Michael D. Beckwith)

were both removed for safety reasons in 1965/66. The building was extensively restored in 1985–86. The Council Chamber on the first floor is wood panelled and has murals painted by J. R. Brown in 1901 depicting the marriage of King Henry VII (of Lancaster) to Princess Elizabeth (of York) in 1486, the surrender of the Jacobite rebels at the Battle of Preston in 1715, and the last charge of King Richard III at Bosworth Field in 1485. The four stained-glass windows in the west-facing elevation represent education, light industry, agriculture and sport, and recreation. There is also a stained-glass window set into the ceiling, which was restored in August 2019.

26. Central Library and Grundy Art Gallery, Queen Street

The library and art gallery were built on land provided by Blackpool Corporation. The library was funded with monies donated by Andrew Carnegie, the Scottish and American philanthropist and officially opened on 26 October 1911. It was designed by Cullen, Lochhead & Brown, architects, in an Edwardian baroque style and is two storey, built in red brick with stone dressings. The corner entrance has a curved colonnade of six Ionic columns surrounded by a balustrade and has an octagonal lead clad dome with urn finial above. There are identical façades facing Queen Street and Abingdon Street. The ground floor houses the main library area,

Above: Central Library and Grundy Art Gallery, Queen Street.

Below: Central Library, September 2020.

including a children's area. There are also public access computers with free access to the internet. Over the doorway is a stained-glass window showing the borough crest. This window was renewed in 1999 as a Millennium gift from the Blackpool Civic Trust. As part of the centenary renovation of the building in 2011, eight stained-glass windows were commissioned and made by Rainbow Glass Studios of London. The first floor houses the Local and Family History Centre, a study area, and meeting and activity rooms.

The adjoining Grundy Art Gallery, on Queen Street, was commissioned by Blackpool Corporation in 1908 and opened in 1911 with the help of a bequest of over twenty paintings and monies from artists Sir Cuthbert and John Grundy. Before 1911, the town's art collection was housed at Revoe Library. The entrance to the art gallery has coupled Ionic columns supporting a stone pediment. The Central Library and Grundy Art Gallery were Grade II listed on 20 October 1983. The Grundy has a rising national and international reputation. Along with the growing permanent collection, it has a high-quality temporary exhibition programme and is recognised as a leading exhibition venue in the north-west.

27. Victoria Hospital, Whinney Heys Road

Originally, Victoria Hospital (established in 1894) was on Whitegate Drive, where the Whitegate Health Centre is today. The foundation stone to the new Victoria Hospital, at Whinney Heys, was laid on 9 June 1933 by Lord Derby

Victoria Hospital, Whinney Heys Road.

Above: A&E, Victoria Hospital.

Below: Rehabilitation Unit, Victoria Hospital.

and opened in 1936. The hospital has developed over the years and is part of the Blackpool Teaching Hospitals NHS Foundation Trust. It has some 767 beds and over 7,000 members of staff. It treats over 100,000 day cases and inpatients and more than 400,000 outpatients every year. Its emergency department is one of the busiest in the country with more than 75,000 attendances every year. It is one of four hospitals in the North West that provides specialist cardiac services in the Lancashire Cardiac Centre.

28. Fire Station, No. 62 Forest Gate

Blackpool Fire Brigade formed in 1858 and was originally located in Hull Street (now within the area of the Hounds Hill Shopping Centre). The fire station moved to Albert Road in 1901 and closed in 1987. The Lancashire Fire & Rescue Service fire station, at No. 62 Forest Gate, which opened 10 April 1987, is manned full time and has two wholetime fire engines and one of the county's three newly developed Rosenbauer aerial ladder platforms. Also housed within the station is the HQ of Western Division covering Blackpool, Bispham, South Shore, Lytham St Annes and Wesham, a technical Fire Safety Enforcement team and a Community Fire Safety team. In addition, the station plays host to Lancashire Blood Bikes.

Fire Station, No. 62 Forest Gate.

29. Moor Park Health and Leisure Centre, Bristol Avenue

The Moor Park Health and Leisure Centre on Bristol Avenue was opened in 2011, at a cost of £12.5 million, on the Moor Park and Bispham Recreation Ground sites. It is a multi-functional building that accommodates community, leisure, sport, education, and healthcare facilities. The main entrance is from Bristol Avenue through the glazed and spacious two-storey atrium, which contains the visitor and patient reception area and a café. The health centre is a three-storey

Above: Moor Park Health and Leisure Centre, Bristol Avenue.

Right: Moor Park Health and Leisure Centre's reception.

building and houses the North Shore Surgery, Glenroyd Medical Centre, Primary Care Trust outpatient services, dental suite, and pharmacy. It incorporates dedicated space for children's services, minor surgery suites, X-ray department and diagnostics, health visitors and district nurses. The two-storey leisure centre houses the existing 25-metre public swimming pool, children's and adults' library (which replaced Bispham Library), sports hall, and, on the first floor, exercise, spinning and fitness studios.

30. Police HQ, Gerry Richardson Way, Marton

The new West Division Police Headquarters on Gerry Richardson Way, off Clifton Road in Marton, officially opened on Wednesday 26 June 2019 and was dedicated to the fallen officers across Blackpool, Fylde, Wyre, Lancaster, and Morecambe. The front counter opened its doors to the public on 23 July 2019. The new headquarters replaces Bonny Street Police Station in central Blackpool, which was built in 1976 and closed in October 2018. The new HQ provides a base for local policing, immediate response, specialist teams, an investigations hub and forty-two custody cells. The three-storey building on the former Progress House site was designed by McBains Cooper Consulting Ltd and built by Willmott Dixon between 2016 and 2018 at a cost of over £20 million. It featured largely in the recent Netflix series titled *Stay Close* starring James Nesbitt.

Police HQ, Gerry Richardson Way, Marton.

Other Buildings around Blackpool

31. Blackpool and The Fylde College

The initial development of the Blackpool and The Fylde College began in Fleetwood at the School for Fishermen in 1892 (later becoming the Nautical College) but it is the Palatine Road site in Blackpool (which opened on 22 November 1937) that was the main site for many years. The college is best known for the provision of courses to support the hotel and catering (hospitality) industry, which are thought to have begun in Blackpool in the 1930s. In the late 1940s a house called Courtfield on the corner of Hornby Road and Park Road was purchased from the Mather family at a cost of £14,750. Courtfield became a centre of excellence for hotel and catering in the UK and provided training from 1947 to 1969. The hotel and catering department then moved to the new site at Bispham but returned to Courtfield between 1986 and 1998. In the 1960s the college was spread over several sites and it was decided to bring these together on one main site. The first building on the Ashfield Road, Bispham, campus site was the seven-storey tower, named the Cleveleys Building, which opened in 1969. This housed the College's

Blackpool and The Fylde College, Ashfield Road, Bispham.

Blackpool and The Fylde College, Palatine Road.

Hotel and Catering Departments with its sixth-floor restaurant in the Machin Room, now the Level 6 restaurant and training kitchens. Phase two of the college development led to the College's Engineering Departments being opened at Easter 1972. The Bispham campus is one of four main campuses located across the Fylde Coast forming the Blackpool and The Fylde College. The college is now able to award Foundation Degrees. It has some 16,000 students annually and over 1,800 local/national companies use the college to deliver education and training programmes for their staff.

32. Bispham Parish Church and Sundial, All Hallows Road

Bispham parish church (also known as All Hallows Church) on All Hallows Road is a Church of England church and is a Grade II listed building. It was Blackpool's parish church until St John's became a parish in 1860. Records show a church was on the site in 1189. The church was rebuilt in 1773 with a choir and musicians gallery, which was entered from steps outside the church. The church was rebuilt again in 1883 to a design by John Lowe of Manchester. The building consists of a five-bay nave, a chancel with transepts and a south-west tower in a minimally Early English style. The inner south doorway is an 1883 restoration of the Norman original, incorporating fragments of the original masonry. The tower was fitted

Above: Bispham parish church, All Hallows Road.

Right: Sundial, Bispham parish church.

with a peal of eight bells as a memorial of thanksgiving following the First World War. The churchyard contains many graves of shipwreck victims. Also buried there is Violet Carson (Ena Sharples of ITV's *Coronation Street*), who lived a few doors away. The lych gate was built in 1901 and is ever popular with photographers. The Grade II listed sundial, located within the graveyard at the south side of the church, is set atop a square shaft, which is mounted on an octagonal stone block that in turn sits on a circular stone disc. The square shaft is believed to be the base of an earlier stone cross. The sundial was designated a Grade II listed building on 20 October 1983. The motto '*Die dies Truditur*' inscribed on the dial translates to 'Day rushes after day'. The inscription is now only partially visible.

33. Water Tower, Leys Road

Blackpool's water tower (1932) and reservoirs (1926) were built by Fylde Water Board on Leys Road (the highest part of Blackpool) on the site of Leys Farm to provide good water supply and pressure to the rapidly expanding town. The water tower, which stands 37.5 metres above ground level, is made of reinforced concrete and faced with pre-cast concrete blocks. The tank at the top of the tower is 7.62 metres deep and holds 114,000 cubic metres of water. Water is pumped to the top of the tower from the two adjacent landscaped/covered reservoirs, which

Water tower, Leys Road.

in turn are fed from Barnacre Reservoir, 16 miles away at Longridge, near Preston. The water tower was owned and run by North West Water Authority from 1973 (later North West Water plc), which merged with NORWEB in December 1995 to form United Utilities.

34. Savoy Garage, No. 2 King Edward Avenue

The Savoy Garage on King Edward Avenue, North Shore, is a Grade II listed building. The garage was designed by T. G. Lumb, Son & Walton of Blackpool and was built in 1914–15 to serve the Savoy Hotel as a covered car park for 100 cars and provide maintenance and repair services. The front elevation is clad with pale buff terracotta incorporating a shaped gable. It was listed on 6 March 2012 as part of English Heritage's Motor Car Project, to recognise the impact of the motor car on the historic environment. It is a rare example of an early covered car park on two levels with a lift. The garage retains many of its original features including a turntable and car lift to the first floor by the Wadsworth Lift Company, Bolton. This remains in working order and retains its original operating and control mechanisms, including the operating handle, which moves between 'ASCEND', 'REST' and 'DESCEND'. It is now a garage run by Peter Drew, with storage on the first floor. A fact about King Edward Avenue, Blackpool, is that in the early 1920s William Lyons and William Walmsley both lived there. From the building of the Swallow sidecars and the Austin Swallow Seven car with Walmsley, William Lyons would go on to create the Jaguar motor company.

Savoy Garage, No. 2 King Edward Avenue.

Savoy Garage's turntable and lift.

35. Queens Park Redevelopment, Layton

Few will remember the Queenstown area (as it was known) before the terraced houses of Wildman Street, St Joseph Road, Gavan Street, Thomas Street, Ward Street and Smith Street were demolished. The seventeen-storey Charles Court, Ashworth Court, Elizabeth Court and Churchill Court tower blocks were built in the 1960s and the twenty-two-storey Walter Robinson Court tower block in 1972. Charles Court and Ashworth Court were demolished in 2014 and the other three tower blocks were dramatically 'blown up' on the afternoon of Sunday 31 July 2016. The award-winning redevelopment of Queens Park, adjacent to Layton Rec, has been completed in phases since 2015 and includes low rise, sustainable apartment blocks, a mix of two, three and four-bedroom homes, public open space, pond and a children's play area.

Above: Queens Park redevelopment, Layton.

Below: Queens Park.

36. Blackpool North Station, Talbot Road

Blackpool's first railway station fronted onto Dickson Road and opened as Blackpool station on 29 April 1846. It was renamed Talbot Road station in 1872 and rebuilt in 1898 in the red brick some will still remember with its glass canopy on Dickson Road. The station was renamed Blackpool North in 1932. The part of the station fronting onto Dickson Road was demolished in 1974 and a Fine Fare supermarket with multistorey car park built on the site. The railway terminus relocated to the 1938 excursion building, previously accessed from Upper Queen Street. The new Blackpool North station, on Talbot Road (as seen below), opened in 1973 and is Blackpool's main railway station. The electrification of the line from Preston in 2018 required track remodelling and signaling work to be carried out. The station was closed for some eighteen weeks, reopening on 16 April 2018. As part of the Talbot Gateway Phase 2 works, the old station site will house a new 4* Holiday Inn and a Marco Pierre White restaurant. Also, an £18 million tramway extension will link North station to the Promenade at Talbot Square, which is planned to be completed in 2022.

Blackpool North station, Talbot Road.

Blackpool North station concourse.

37. Funny Girls (formerly the Odeon Cinema), Dickson Road

The iconic art deco building on Dickson Road opened on 6 May 1939 as the Odeon Cinema and is a Grade II listed building. It is a steel frame building clad in cream and green faience to the front elevation and black faience to lower part of the left side (Springfield Road) elevation under the original queue canopy. It had a large 'ODEON' sign in red lettering to the front elevation and to all four sides of the corner tower. This has been changed and the signs now read 'FUNNY GIRLS'. The auditorium originally had accommodation for 3,000 in the stalls and single circle, with foyers on both levels. The cinema was subdivided in 1975 to form three smaller cinemas. It closed as a cinema in 1998 and was opened by actress Joan Collins in July 2002 as Pink Leisure's 'Funny Girls Showbar', featuring burlesque cabaret, with the Flamingo nightclub accessed from Queen Street. The Funny Girls theatre is in the stalls area of the former cinema and the Flamingo nightclub is in the former Circle, with a bar in the former Circle foyer.

Above: Funny Girls, Dickson Road (formerly the Odeon Cinema).

Below: Funny Girls entrance, Dickson Road.

38. General Post Office (GPO) and its 8 'K6' telephone boxes, Nos 26–30
Abingdon Street

The Renaissance-style GPO building on Abingdon Street was built in 1910 by
R. Neill & Son of Manchester and is now a Grade II listed building. It has three
storeys and cellars. Its impressive façade to the Abingdon Street elevation is
faced with white Portland stone and the rectangular building has a hipped roof
of green slate. The post office had a 70-foot- (21-metre-) long horseshoe counter
in polished mahogany and desk space under the windows for writing of letters,
cheques, and postcards. The main public area also had a marble mosaic floor.
At the rear of the building was the post office's sorting office and telephone
exchange, accessed from Edward Street. The post office was in use until 2007
when it closed and the counter service moved to WHSmith on Bank Hey Street
and is now located at Bickerstaffe House. The sorting office moved to the new
£7 million Royal Mail Delivery Centre, off Faraday Way, in Bispham in 2015.
The eight cast-iron, K6 type, currant red telephone kiosks outside the GPO
building are also Grade II listed and were designed by Sir Giles Gilbert Scott in
1935. Plans have been submitted to convert the former main post office into a
hotel, with shops, a bar, restaurant and roof terrace.

Former General Post Office (GPO), Abingdon Street.

GPO's eight red K6 telephone boxes.

39. Abingdon Street Market

From 1862 to May 1893 this was the site of Blackpool's police station, with offices, a courthouse and three dwelling houses. The building was bought by T. H. Smith, a joiner and builder, who added a storey and the mock-Tudor façade that we see today fronting Abingdon Street. In the early 1900s it was Jackson's Garage, with workshops and a car showroom. It first became the Blackpool Market around 1925 and opened on 4 June 1927 as Abingdon Street Market. Originally there was a central thoroughfare for horse and cart access through to Cedar Square, with a large lantern at the Abingdon Street entrance suspended from ornate ironwork. The first female Mayor of Blackpool (1968–69) was Alderman Jean Robinson JP, CBE. Jean ran the café in the market for twenty-seven years. The market was refurbished in 2012 and the mock-Tudor façade and shop fronts restored. It was owned by TCS Holdings of Leeds until recently and was bought by Blackpool Council in 2020 after it received a £3.6 million grant from the government's Getting Building Fund. Plans have been approved for the renovation and modernisation of the market including a 250-seat food and beverage quarter. The rooms above the market building fronting onto Abingdon Street are now contemporary visual art studios and project space named Abingdon Studios.

Above: Abingdon Street Market.

Below: Abingdon Street Market stalls.

40. St John's Church, St John's Square, Church Street

The first church on this site was built in 1821 as a chapel of ease to the parish church at Bispham and was dedicated to John the Evangelist. It was enlarged in 1832 and again in 1847. A chancel was added in 1851. It became Blackpool's Anglican parish church in 1860. The churchyard on Church Street was closed to burials when Layton Cemetery opened in 1873. The church was found to be too small for Blackpool's rapidly expanding population and it was demolished. The present church was built in 1877 and consecrated in 1878. The present Grade II listed church was designed by Garlick, Park and Sykes and the foundation stone was laid by Blackpool's first mayor, Dr William Cocker. St John's Church is built of yellow stone with a slate roof and is in the Early English style. The tower has four stages, angled buttresses, two belfry louvres on each side and is topped with pinnacles and finials. The inside is in ashlar. Restoration work was carried out in 1986, with further restoration between 2000 and 2006, at a cost

St John's Church, St John's Square.

Worship area, St John's Church.

of £1.6 million. The church interior has been completely remodelled and a new worship area created together with versatile spaces able to be used by the church and community. A two-storey emergency shelter for homeless young people was created and is attached to the west end of the church. The shelter is run by Streetlife Trust and provides overnight accommodation to sleep ten people on the first floor. St John's has a full-time children and families' pastor and a youth and digital pastor. In February 2019, the CLC Christian book shop, formerly on Abingdon Street, moved into the church and the shop is normally open six days a week alongside the small heritage centre.

41. Houndshill Shopping Centre

Planning for a covered shopping centre in the Hounds Hill area of town began in the early 1960s. The Houndshill Shopping Centre opened in 1980, bounded by Victoria Street, Bank Hey Street, Adelaide Street and Coronation Street. The new shopping centre and four-storey car park was built over Sefton Street, Water Street, Board Street and Tower Street. It replaced the Congregational Chapel of 1849 on Victoria Street as well as a myriad of small and aged shops and properties. It also necessitated the demolition of Brian London's famous 007 nightclub on Tower Street. The shopping centre was extended to Albert Road and opened in September 2008 with Debenhams as the new anchor store, trebling the size of the shopping centre. Debenhams closed on 8 May 2021.

Above: Houndshill Shopping Centre's Victoria Street entrance.

Below: Houndshill Shopping Centre.

Above: Houndshill's Adelaide Street entrance.

Below: The former Debenhams, Houndshill, on the junction of Coronation Street and Albert Road.

Hounds Hill Shopping Centre was bought by BCC Eiffel in 2015 but they went into receivership in 2019 and the shopping centre was acquired by Blackpool Council for £47 million. A further extension is under construction on the Coronation Street/Tower Street car park area (opposite the Olympia), planned for completion in winter 2022, which will include an 850-seat IMAX cinema, multimedia entertainment centre and a Wilko store.

42. Raikes Hall, Liverpool Road

Raikes Hall is a Grade II listed building with a Georgian exterior uncommon in Blackpool. It was built around 1764 by Willian Butcher/Boucher. The house was initially built as a gentleman's residence with three parlours on the ground floor, four lodging rooms upstairs, a servant's hall, butcher's pantry and kitchen, servant quarters, stables, orchards and gardens. After William Boucher's death in 1797, the hall was later sold to William Hornby in 1802. It was leased to the Sisters of the Holy Child Jesus in 1859 and became a convent girls' school until the lease ran out in 1870, when it was sold to the Raikes Hall Park, Gardens and Aquarium Company, who developed its 51-acre site as the principal tourist attraction of Blackpool prior to the Winter Gardens and Tower opening. It was later known as the Royal Palace Gardens. Raikes Hall itself was sold by Burnley brewers Massey's to Catterall & Swarbrick

Raikes Hall, Liverpool Road.

Raikes Hall and its bowling green.

Brewery Ltd in 1930 and is now a traditional pub owned by Trust Inns, with a large lounge and bar area, a meeting room upstairs, a large beer garden and privately run bowling green.

43. Grange Park

Grange Park is a large council-built housing estate to the east of St Walburgas Road. Its name comes from Grange Farm, which stood in the hamlet of Little Layton. Whilst around 140 'Prefabs' were built after the end of the Second World War, the first of some 1,800 dwellings were built in 1946. It was classed as a socially deprived area for many years and in April 1997 the Grange Park Initiative project was established to improve the estate.

Grange Park was previously served by shops at Dinmore Place, Chepstow Road and Easington Crescent, as well as the Dinmore Hotel pub on Dinmore Avenue, which opened in 1963. In recent years all the shops have been demolished and some have been relocated from Chepstow Road to The Grange. The Dinmore pub closed in 2013 and was demolished 2017. The City Learning Centre, on the corner of Bathurst Avenue and Dinmore Avenue, was built around 2003. It was redeveloped in 2017 and renamed The Grange. The Grange is the community hub for Grange Park and is the home of the Community Farm, the Boundary Library, Community Café, HIS provision Community Shop, the Grange Pharmacy and the One Stop Shop. It also has community rooms for hire as well as a large Theatre space. In addition to The Grange, the estate also has Argosy Court Community Centre and Horsebridge Community Centre.

The Grange, Grange Park.

Grange Park Primary School on Dinmore Avenue was built in 1953 and closed in 2001. The building was used in 2004–06 to accommodate the pupils from Devonshire Road Junior School after the fire there on 23 August 2003. It was succeeded by Boundary Primary School in 2003. St Catherine's (girls) and St Thomas of Canterbury (boys) Roman Catholic Secondary Schools opened on Yew Tree Road in 1963 and 1968, respectively. The two schools merged to become All Saints Roman Catholic High School and the school closed in 1982 when it merged with St Mary's Catholic College. In 1996, the buildings were replaced with housing. Catholic mass at Grange Park was first held in a converted cowshed in the grounds of Layton Hill Convent until Christ the King Church opened on Chepstow Road in 1954. An infant school in a wooden building opened behind the church in 1958 and was replaced by a new school on Bathurst Avenue in 1973. The church and school were relocated to Rodwell Walk in September 2015. St Michael and All Angels Church of England Church, at Calvert Place, opened in 1958. It closed in 2004 with the site being used for housing.

The partners at Bloomfield Medical Centre, on Bloomfield Road, have joined forces with the former Dinmore Avenue Surgery to form the Grange Park Health Centre on Dinmore Avenue. The former Hoyle House nursing home on Argosy Avenue closed in 2013 and was demolished in 2016. The site has been developed with a mix of bungalows and houses. Grange Park Children's Centre on Dingle Avenue helps provide children with the best start in life and also provides advice on

Above: Boundary Primary School, Grange Park.

Below: Dinmore Avenue at Tarnbrook Drive, Grange Park.

Fulwood Avenue, Grange Park.

health, family matters, training and job opportunities. Boundary Park on Argosy Avenue has playing fields and children's play area. The park is the home of FC Rangers Junior Football Club, which formed in 1970. Gateside Park on Chepstow Road underwent a major revamp in 2019 including new paths, drainage, picnic area and wooden carved archways at the entrances.

44. Blackpool Zoo, East Park Drive

Blackpool Zoo opened on 6 July 1972 on East Park Drive. The site was formerly Blackpool Municipal Airport, which opened in 1929 and was requisitioned during the Second World War for use by the Royal Air Force. It closed in 1947, after which it hosted the annual Royal Lancashire Agricultural Show until 1970. Some of the original airport buildings were utilised by the zoo, with one converted into the elephant house and a hangar later converted to become the new entrance, with shops. The zoo has 1,500 animals and thirty life-size dinosaur models in the Dinosaur Safari, which was completed in 2005. The zoo is home to six Asian elephants. The first elephant was Kate, who arrived in 1972 and was later joined byTara, Minbu, Noorjahan, Esha and Emmett. In 2017 a new elephant house and paddock was opened when Project Elephant Base Camp was completed. The zoo also houses a female Amur (Siberian) tiger, Alyon, who now lives on her own since the passing of her mate, Zambar, in 2018. Gorilla Mountain opened in 2000 and is home to six Western Lowland gorillas. The zoo has two male African lions, Wallace and his son Khari, who was born in 2015. Orangutan Outlook was completed in 2014 and is the home of the zoo's Bornean orangutans.

Above: Blackpool Zoo's East Park Drive entrance.

Below: Blackpool Zoo (former airport control tower).

Above: The Giraffe House, Blackpool Zoo.

Below: The Elephant House, Blackpool Zoo.

More recent developments include the new giraffe enclosure, with its high-level viewing platform, opened in 2008, the Magellanic penguin enclosure in 2009 and the refurbished California sea lion pool (the largest in Britain) with its glass viewing walls and a 300-seat grandstand, which opened in May 2010. The zoo has an excellent children's farm, which opened in 2011. It also has a 15-inch-gauge miniature railway (1972) that runs for over 600 metres along the western and northern edges of the zoo. The zoo has been owned and run since 2007 by Parques Reunidos, a Spanish-based leisure organisation.

45. Revoe Library and Gymnasium, Central Drive

The area of Revoe was farmland until the 1860s with few roads. However, with the rapid development and expansion of Blackpool, the farms were sold to developers. In 1882, Central Drive ran as far as Revoe Farm and was extended to Waterloo Road in the mid-1890s. In 1891, the remains of Revoe Farm, which stood generally where Revoe Library stands today, were sold to Dr W. H. Cocker's Cleveleys Estate Company for £1,700. In 1900, the Corporation applied to borrow £1,050 to purchase land at Revoe and to build a library and gymnasium.

Revoe Library and Gymnasium, Central Drive.

Revoe Farm was demolished in 1901. The new library opened on 23 July 1904 and the gymnasium opened on 6 October 1904. Blackpool Keidokwai Judo Club was established in 1942 and utilises the gymnasium above the library.

46. Blackpool Football Club, Bloomfield Road

Blackpool Football Club, as we know it today, was founded on 26 July 1887. In its early years it played at Raikes Hall Gardens and also at the Athletic Grounds, which was near the present-day Blackpool Cricket Club. The football club merged with South Shore Football Club on 21 December 1899 and played its first game at Bloomfield Road against Horwich RMI on 23 December 1899, winning 8-0. At that date, the ground had a small wooden stand along the western side of the pitch, which could hold 300 spectators, and a perimeter fence to keep spectators off the pitch. The facilities at the ground slowly developed over the years. A new two-tiered South Stand opened in 1925, which survived until it was demolished in 2002–03 and a new West Stand opened on 31 August 1929. The North Terrace (Spion Kop) opened on 30 August 1930 and was originally (in the 1930s and 1940s) a grassy slope with railway sleepers on it. It was concreted and terraced (and further enlarged) for the 1950 season, increasing the ground's capacity to over 30,000. In the 1980s the capacity of the ground was gradually reduced to under 10,000 and the western half of the Kop was closed, with the eastern half open only to visiting supporters. The Kop and West Stand were demolished in 2000 and 2001, respectively, to make way for new stands.

South Stand, Blackpool Football Club, Bloomfield Road.

Today, the new West Stand is the main stand and is named after the great Sir Stanley Matthews. It was officially opened on 6 August 2002 at the same time as the new North Stand. The player's tunnel has been relocated to the West Stand from the South Stand abutting Bloomfield Road, from where the ground gets its name. The West Stand houses the main reception as well as the club's offices. The North Stand is named after Stan Mortensen, who died on 22 May 1991. A statue of him was unveiled outside the North Stand by his widow in 2005. The North Stand also houses the Safehands Green Start Nursery and offices for Blackpool Primary Care Trust. The new South Stand was opened in March 2010 by Valeri Belokon and Jimmy Armfield. It also houses a hotel and a restaurant named Rowley's. The new South Stand is named the Jimmy Armfield Stand after the Blackpool and England captain. A 9-feet-tall bronze statue of Jimmy Armfield CBE DL was unveiled in front of his stand on 1 May 2011, exactly forty years after he retired from playing. The East Stand was formerly known as the East Paddock or locally the 'Scratching Shed'. It was replaced by a temporary stand built in 2010 to bring the ground up to the standard required for the club's debut season in the Premier League and is used by away fans.

47. Saddle Inn, No. 286 Whitegate Drive, Marton

The Saddle Inn on the corner of Whitegate Drive and Preston Old Road, at Great Marton, dates from around 1776, when it was owned by Richard Hall, a saddler of Little Marton. In 1814, it was owned by Thomas Crook, a maltster of Great Marton, and known as the 'Roundabout House', as the front door was at the back of the pub where the kitchen extension is now. In 1892, William and Eliza Leigh were landlords at the Saddle and their descendants were landlords until Jim (James Shepherd Leigh – the Beekeeper) retired in 1967. Besides the bar and entrance areas there were three separate rooms each with their own historical names. There was the tiny 'House of Lords' room at the front, which was a 'men-only' snug until the enactment of the Sex Discrimination Act of 1975, with its red leather bench seating and pictures of the former members of Marton Council, who used to meet in the room. The 'Smoke-Room,' with its stained-glass panel above the doorway, blue carpeting and oil paintings of sailing ships, was the front lounge. It was converted to a no-smoking room in the 1970s and as food was served in the room, dogs were banned. The long back room with its green-coloured bench seating and pictures of past sporting heroes is still called the 'Commons' and is now the domain of the pub's regulars. The pub was owned by Catterall & Swarbrick [C&S] until 1961 when they were bought by Northern Breweries of Great Britain Ltd, who merged with Bass Charrington. Bass changed the original layout of the pub by removing the wall separating the bar area and the 'Lords' room and developed the outside beer garden and play area from 1992. Don and Pam Ashton started the annual Saddle Beer Festival in 1994 in a marque adjacent to the pub. The Saddle is now owned by the Stonegate Pub Company Limited.

Above: Saddle Inn, No. 286 Whitegate Drive, Marton.

Below: Saddle Inn bar.

48. Marton Institute, Oxford Square

Marton Working Men's Club and Institute (as it was originally named) is a private members' club at Oxford Square. The club was founded in 1895 by a group chaired by Mr J. P. Dixon to provide recreational facilities for the men and women of Marton village. The building fund came from a £500 donation by Mr James Parrott, a loan from Lancashire and Yorkshire Bank and the Ladies' Committee, who held a bazaar to raise money for the benefit of the institute. Mr Parrott (then ninety-three years old) laid the foundation stone on 27 April 1895 and the institute opened on 8 December 1897. Facilities at the club originally included a main club room and a large entertainment room able to seat 300 people. There was also a room used for the institute's band to practise and a reading room. Upstairs was the billiard and games room and at the rear was the bowling green. The building has been extended and today the facilities include a self-contained function suite, first-floor games room, beer garden, a crown green bowling green and a car park. A marque is erected in the car park for the annual beer and music festival.

Marton Institute,
Oxford Square.

49. Little Marton Mill, Preston New Road

Standing on a raised green on Preston New Road, Little Marton Mill was built in 1838 by millwright Richard Blezard. It was a gristmill, designed for grinding grain (corn) and stands on the site of a previous tower mill, which in turn was the site of a yet earlier post mill. The mill was owned by the Clifton Estate and originally leased to Nancy Whalley and her son John. It is a three-storey circular tower mill with basement and is built of brick with white-painted external rendering. The entrance to the mill is through double doors to the east, at basement level, and a single door to the west. There are square windows at the first, second and third storeys. Its roof (replaced in 1986) is a clinker-built upturned boat shape and there are four dummy sails and a fantail with eight blades. Some original machinery remains on the second floor. The upper-floor houses a vertical shaft and cogged wheel known as a wallower and a wind shaft that carries the external sails. There is also machinery that turned the cap on the mill to bring the sails into the wind.

Little Marton Mill, Preston New Road.

The mill was purchased by the Bagot family in 1922, with Cornelius Bagot becoming the miller, but production ceased in September 1928. In 1937, after restoration, Cornelius gifted the mill, in trust, to be maintained as a memorial to his friend Allen Clarke, who was a noted local historian, author and windmill enthusiast. Cornelius tragically died on his birthday in 1940 when he was knocked down by a taxi during a Second World War blackout. In 1953, the mill was tenanted by the Shepherd family, who used the mill building for the manufacture of poultry machinery. It later became headquarters of the 53rd Blackpool Scout Group. The mill became a Grade II listed building on 20 October 1983 and was renovated in 1987 at a cost of £88,000. It is the only mill left standing within Blackpool and is preserved by the Friends of Little Marton Mill, who hold open days.

5c. The Cottage at Blowing Sands, No. 166 Common Edge Road, Marton Moss

After the draining of the Marton Moss area in the mid-seventeenth century, farming of the area became possible and cottages began to be built. The white cottage in the picture, at No. 166 Common Edge Road, close to the junction with Squires Gate Lane and Progress Way is in the area known locally as Blowing Sands. The building was probably two agricultural cottages originally. It has two low storeys to the front and is constructed from brick and cobbles with a slate roof. It remains representative of the several cottages that were built in the area and is a Grade II listed building.

The Cottage at Blowing Sands, No. 166 Common Edge Road, Marton.

Sources and Acknowledgements

Michael D. Beckwith, Gregg Wolstenholme, Mark Spencer, Historic England, Eva Byrant, Blackpool and The Fylde College, Claire Frost, Stephanie Taylor, Imperial Hotel, Stephanie Evans, Blackpool Pleasure Beach, Robert Owen, Institution of Civil Engineers, Panel for Historical Engineering, Carol Morgan, Merlin Entertainments Limited, Jade Sawden, Blackpool Entertainment Company Ltd, Anthony Williams, D. Thorley (Pixabay), Tony Sharkey, Ted Lightbown, Antony Hill, SM Malcolm Dewhurst of the Lancashire Fire and Rescue Service, Patrick Thompson, Blackpool Central Library, Professor Vanessa Toulmin, Blackpool Council, https://www.blackpool.gov.uk/Residents/Planning-environment-and-community/Planning/Conservation/Blackpool-locally-listed-buildings.aspx, http://www.blackpoolcivictrust.org.uk, liveBlackpool, Wikipedia, Nick Moore, Peter Drew, Revd Steve Haskett of St John's Church, Ann Banks, Howard Deane, Lancashire Online Parish Clerks, Canon Bob Dewhurst of Sacred Heart Church, Jo and Richard Schwab, Neil at Roberts' Oyster Bar, Blackpool Zoo, Della Belk. Michelle Wood, Annie Gilbert, Andy Gent, Keith Roberts, Chris and Alex Wood, Clare Wood, Norma Fowden, Linda Edgar, Rachel and Becky Bottomley, Stan Jefferies, Dave Heaney, David Grove and Gerry Wolstenholme.

Allan and Chris at Roberts Oyster Bar.